To Emilie Chandler

As long as the earth endures, seedtime and harvest, cold and heat,
summer and winter, day and night will never cease.   Genesis 8:22

Copyright © 1996 by Educational Publishing Concepts, Inc., Wheaton, Illinois

Published by Concordia Publishing House
3558 S. Jefferson Avenue, St. Louis, MO 63118-3968
Manufactured in the United States of America

1 2 3 4 5 6 7 8 9 10   05 04 03 02 01 00 99 98 97 96

Sand and Shells Carousels Silver Bells

by Isabel Anders
Illustrated by Rick Incrocci

CPH
SAINT LOUIS

A Blank Page to Write On

I love to write on paper
  And fill the empty space,
To draw my house with windowpanes
  And add a happy face.

I scribble all the things I want
  And what I'm going to do.
Or I'll make paper airplanes fly
  And roll a scroll or two.

And now this fresh year gives me
  The chance to start out new
With words and thoughts and actions
  That honor what is true.

I'm sort of like blank paper–
  With a message on my face.
Lord, help me to write carefully
  And always give You space

To write the things upon my life
  That You wish to be there.
Make me a "letter" to the world
  To show Your love and care.

You are a letter from Christ . . . written not with ink but with the Spirit of the living God, not on tablets of stone but on tablets of human hearts.

2 Corinthians 3:3

Winter Pleasures

I love the world in winter
    And always wait to see
The snow in all its whiteness
    Fall on every rock and tree.

On mornings, objects glisten
    With frost like glitter bright.
I never could imagine it
    While sleeping through the night!

I reach for warmer clothes,
    And add my mittens too,
To hold myself against the wind
    Although the sky's so blue!

God sets the stage this season–
    And hurls the hail to earth!
I love to watch the ice and snow
    While sitting by the hearth.

Lord, make me thankful for each day,
    Whatever it may bring.
Then even bitter winter days
    Can seem as fine as spring!

He spreads the snow like wool and scatters the frost like ashes. He hurls down His hail like pebbles. Who can withstand His icy blast? He sends His word and melts them; He stirs up His breezes, and the waters flow.

Psalm 147:16-18

Catch the Wind

Who can stop the wind
    From sweeping through the trees?
It runs right through my fingers
    And always seems to tease.

I hold my cap on tightly
    And brace myself to race
Directly to the bus stop
    And try to stay in place.

Though we can't see the wind itself
    We know what it can do
To keep the world in motion–
    Blowing down a thing or two!

Lord, I'm sure Your mighty power
    Is greater than the wind.
You made the earth so large and great
    To place Your people in.

I watch the stars at night,
    Thinking of Your heavenly place.
But by day the clouds, like cotton,
    Always seem to hide Your face.

Yet every time I ponder
    The great, wide sky above–
The seas that spread, the land so vast–
    I celebrate Your love.

Lord, show me every day
    The way my life should be.
Though I'll never catch the wind
    I can feel Your love for me!

He makes the clouds His chariot and rides on the wings of the wind.
Psalm 104:3

It's Easter in My Heart

It's Easter in my heart.
I know that Jesus lives.
His presence in my life
Brings a power that gives—and gives!

It's Easter in my heart
And God shows me how to pray.
I kneel down in the morning
And at the close of day.

It's Easter in my heart
And God helps me answer "No!"
To lying, fears, and pathways
Where it isn't safe to go.

It's Easter in my heart
And God helps me give to others—
My time, and smiles . . . and
Listen to my sisters and brothers.

It's Easter in my heart
And God gives me peace within,
A heart that's filled with faith,
And the strength to turn from sin.

It's Easter in my heart
And I wake each day with praise.
With thanks to God that Jesus lives,
My voice I'll gladly raise!

Lord, let Easter bloom within my heart
And last throughout the year.
Then I can face what each day brings,
Rejoicing without fear.

Praise be to the God and Father of our Lord Jesus Christ! In His great mercy He has given us new birth into a living hope through the resurrection of Jesus Christ from the dead.
1 Peter 1:3

At the Fair

The winds die down in April.
     Spring is coming, we can tell!
One day we take a ride
     On a swift, bright carousel.

I love to hug my stallion,
     Gripping its firm mane.
I'll ride into the sunset,
     Down a crooked lane.

I make-believe I'm going West
     To take my cattle home.
I close my eyes and concentrate,
     Pretending I'm alone.

It's fun just to imagine,
     While I'm whirling like a ball,
The things that I'll do later
     When I grow up big and tall.

But soon the ride is over
    And I step down from my steed.
Someday I'll find adventure
    And all the things I need.

Lord, keep me safe and trusting
    In everything I do,
So—fast or slow—I'm staying close
    And giving thanks to You.

Like a horse in open country, they did not stumble; like cattle that go down to the plain, they were given rest by the Spirit of the Lord.

Isaiah 63:13-14

Flowersong

God has a palette
          With a range
Of colors—oh, so bright!

In May the world
          Has felt God's brush,
Each flower painted right!

The sky above
          Gives perfect depth
To wonders high and low.

God is the artist
          Who's been here
Delighting us, I know.

And so I'll sing
          A flowersong
For rose and daffodil,

For pansy, buttercup,
          And for
The grass on every hill!

The beauty of the spring
      Makes my heart
Soar like a bird.

Lord, I know this
      Special season has
A promise in Your Word.

And so I'll shout
      It everywhere:
Be happy! Spring is here!

The God who saves
      Has blessed us with
The springtime of the year.

Flowers appear on the earth; the season of singing has come, the cooing of doves is heard in our land.

Song of Songs 2:12

Sand and Shells

Summer days are longer,
    And we have more time to play.
My favorite place is at the beach.
    I always want to stay!

I watch my feet make prints
    In the soft and yielding sand
And wade into the water
    Where it laps up to the land.

I gather many shells
    And take them home to keep:
Whelk and conch and scallop–
    My treasures from the deep!

I sometimes wish that summer
    Could last throughout the year.
As I count my shells and shake out sand
    And see the water clear.

Lord, keep me in Your goodness.
    Let me count the stars at night
Until I just lose count,
    Resting, sleeping, in Your sight.

I will surely bless you and make your descendants as numerous as the stars in the sky and as the sand on the seashore . . . And through your offspring all nations on earth will be blessed.

Genesis 22:17

Thunderclaps

July brings heat
   That seems to cause
A sudden change outdoors.
   Just when the sky
   Is still and
Dark . . .

Suddenly–
Thunder roars!

I gather up my toys
   And bring them all
Inside.
The rain hits
   Oh, so
Forcefully–

As though a
Giant cried!

But I know that
   Even rain
And lightning in the sky
Are all part of
   God's greatness–

Although we wonder why . . .

We can't run from
     The thunderclaps
So noisy up above.
     And we never can escape
     From God
Who shelters us with love.

And so I say a special
     Prayer
Inside, while safe and dry.

Lord, thank You for
     Your power
That keeps me wondering "why?"

Listen! Listen to the roar of His voice, to the rumbling that comes from His mouth. He unleashes His lightning beneath the whole heaven and sends it to the ends of the earth . . . God's voice thunders in marvelous ways; He does great things beyond our understanding.

Job 37:2-3, 5

The Sun in All Its Brightness

The morning sun that wakes me up
    Is such a friendly sight.
It's easier to start the day
    Beneath its smile so bright.

The sunlight warms my shoulders
    As I play throughout the day.
And then at night I miss its glow–
    I wish that it would stay!

But Mr. Sun's a daytime friend.
    God placed it up above
To give us warmth and light that
    Can remind us of His love.

We cannot look right at the sun
    Or measure its great size.
Its dazzling light is just too great
    To take in with our eyes.

God gave the sun a special place,
    Important work to do,
And blessed our earth with all the range
    Of heat and coldness too.

On August days I think of snow–
    Its cold and icy touch.
But I like sun and summer fun
    Every bit as much!

So, the sun in all its brightness
    I'll give thanks for every night.
Lord, may the sun remind my heart
    Of Your goodness and Your might.

Now no one can look at the sun, bright as it is in the skies after the wind has swept them clean.
Out of the north He comes in golden splendor; God comes in awesome majesty.

Job 37:21-22

From a Tiny Seed

When you plant a simple seed
　　　You wonder, "Will it be
A flower, or a mighty oak
　　　To shelter you and me?"

You dig a circle in the earth
　　　And place your seed inside.
Then you cover it with dirt
　　　Where it can grow and hide.

The rains that come, the sun and warmth,
　　　Can do amazing things.
Suddenly one day you know
　　　The joy that planting brings.

First there is a little green
　　　Emerging from the ground.
Then, soon, a stem, though very small–
　　　Amazingly–you've found.

Will you have a flower that
　　　The bees can gather 'round?
Or is this stem the first growth of
　　　The largest tree in town?

I think that all this planting
    Is sort of like kind deeds.
God helps you share His love in Christ
    and help with someone's needs.

Growing things are all around us.
    Yet not till winter's here
Will we know what plants can make it through
    The coldness of the year.

Lord, help me share in words and acts
    The Good News of Your Son.
Lord, may my life be like a tree
    With many new souls won.

The kingdom of heaven is like a mustard seed . . . Though it is the smallest of all your seeds, yet when it grows, it is the largest of garden plants and becomes a tree, so that the birds of the air come and perch in its branches.

Matthew 13:31-32

Giving God Our Best

Today we're having company–
    The house is sparkling bright!
The kitchen air is full of smells
    That give my nose delight!

We've set our finest dishes
    Upon the dining table.
I do my part with little tasks,
    Helping as I'm able.

I carry out the garbage
    And straighten up the place.
But most of all I dress up nice
    And wear a happy face!

We want to welcome guests
    With love and kindness here.
I'm glad to join the party
    And to celebrate with cheer.

But Mom says every day we sit
    And thank God for our food
Is special too–and teaches us
    A lesson for our good.

So whether we have fancy meals
And sparkling punch to drink,
Or simple, everyday good food,
It always makes me think

How God invites all to a meal–
The greatest and the least.
Christ's love is what we take inside
At God's great banquet feast.

And so in celebration,
Lord, let me learn today
To keep Your loving care in mind
While I eat, or work, or play.

He has taken me to the banquet hall, and His banner over me is love.

Song of Songs 2:4

The Thankful Season

I'm thankful in this season
    For all that God has done–
For skies and trees and even for
    These days with little sun.

Although it's dark outside,
    It's warm and cozy here
Beside the fire with family at
    This special time of year.

Lord, show me how each day is like
    A package wrapped up bright,
Waiting to be opened–
    A gift that's always right!

Thanksgiving Day approaches,
    And so I'll list today,
The things to give You thanks for.
    I know that I can say:

Most of all I'm thankful
    To be Your child and know it!
You make my life so rich and good,
    I really want to show it!

Lord, let my faith grow stronger
    As I travel through the days.
Each season calls me in some way
    To give You love and praise!

I always thank God for you because of His grace given you in Christ Jesus. For in Him you have been enriched in every way.

1 Corinthians 1:4-5

The Earth Has Made Its Yearly Course

The earth has made its yearly course–
Now January's near.
It's time to start all over now
And face another year.

One thing we're told within God's Word:
The seasons are the same.
God promised it so long ago–
That some things will remain.

And so throughout the coming days,
In rain or sun or snow,
I feast my eyes on splendors bright
And it's because I know

You are the Lord of all the earth;
You sing creation's song!
Lord, give me eyes to see, and ears
To hear, a voice to sing along!

*As long as the earth endures, seedtime
and harvest, cold and heat, summer and winter,
day and night will never cease.*
Genesis 8:22

Ring Out the Bells

The countdown days to Christmas have begun
　　　　And everywhere I hear the sounds so clear:
Silver bells that echo in the night
　　　　And happy voices whispering, "It's near!"

I decorate my room with bows and wreaths
　　　　And help to make our tree look, oh, so bright.
And when we walk down avenues and streets,
　　　　We wander in the glow of sparkling light.

Lord, help me to remember that these days
　　　　Are filled with more than presents, food, and toys.
Let my voice welcome Your Son in praise–
　　　　And open up my heart to Christmas joys.

For once, so long ago in Bethlehem,
　　　　A King was born–He was a baby, fair.
And someday soon all knees will surely bow
　　　　To this One, who yet a crown will wear.

Help me to give my life in humble ways–
　　　　To add to this great symphony, my song.
And so, as days grow short, I pray, Lord Jesus,
　　　　Come, and do not let us wait too long.

Our hearts are open and our voices ready.
　　　　We want to tell the world about Your birth.
So in this time of giving to each other,
　　　　May alleluias rise o'er all the earth!

Shout for joy to the Lord, all the earth, burst into jubilant song with music; make music to the Lord with the harp, with the harp and the sound of singing, with trumpets and the blast of the ram's horn—shout for joy before the Lord, the King.

Psalm 98:4-6